MONEY MATTERS MADE EASY

A Practical Guide to Financial Empowerment.

George T.Y

Table of content

Introduction

Learning the art of money management is crucial in a society where financial decisions have a significant influence on our lives. Your compass through the complicated world of personal finance is "Money Matters Made Easy: A Practical Guide to Financial Empowerment". This book provides a thorough and user-friendly road map to assist you in reaching your financial objectives, whether you are just beginning your financial journey or wanting to improve your present tactics.

Join us as we debunk the frequently mysterious world of saving, investing, and other topics. This manual offers useful guidance that crosses age, wealth, and background with a focus on pragmatism. You'll discover how to make decisions that set the groundwork for a secure and happy life via accessible examples, expert insights, and real-world success stories.

"Money Matters Made Easy" gives you the information and confidence to take charge of your financial future, from understanding credit ratings to navigating the world of investment alternatives. This book is intended to enable you to make decisions that are in line with your ambitions, whether they involve purchasing a home, launching a company, or simply finding peace of mind, regardless of your present level of financial literacy. Get ready to start a trip that will change the way you see money. As you negotiate the complexity of finance and prepare the way for a better, more successful tomorrow, let "Money Matters Made Easy: A Practical Guide to Financial Empowerment" serve as your compass. The control over your finances begins right now.

Why Financial Empowerment is Important?

Financial empowerment is essential because it gives people the information, abilities, and tools they need to take charge of their financial situation. Making educated decisions about spending, saving, investing, budgeting, and debt management helps people achieve more financial stability and security. This empowerment can eliminate poverty cycles, lessen stress, and increase a feeling of freedom. In the end, having financial independence enables people to pursue their objectives, cope with unforeseen costs, and have a more secure future.

Chapter 1

Building a Strong Financial Foundation.

Building a solid financial foundation entails the following crucial steps:

Establish Specific Objectives: Specify both short- and long-term financial objectives, such as emergency fund accumulation, home purchase, or retirement.

Establish a Budget: To make a practical budget, keep track of your earnings and outgoings. Set aside money for savings, debt repayment, discretionary spending, and basic expenses.

Emergency funds: Create an emergency fund with three to six months' worth of living costs. This serves as a backup plan for unforeseen circumstances.

Manage Debt: Pay off high-interest debts first as a matter of priority. Reduce new debt to a minimum, and if advantageous, consolidate or restructure current debt.

Saving and investment: Consistently save money and make smart investments. Based on your time horizon and risk tolerance, diversify your investing portfolio.

Retirement planning :Contribute to retirement funds like 401(k)s or IRAs as part of your retirement planning. To gain from compound growth, start early.

Insurance Protection: To guard against unforeseen financial losses, make sure you have enough coverage for your health, life, and property.

Live Within Your Means and refrain from impulsive purchases. Maintain your spending plan to prevent needless debt.

Continuous Learning: Get personal finance education. Keep current with tax laws, money management skills, and investment strategies.

Regular Reviews: Review and modify your financial strategy on a regular basis. As your circumstances in life change, so should your financial plan.

Estate Planning :To make sure your loved ones are taken care of, make a will, choose beneficiaries, and make provisions for passing on assets.

Professional Help: Take into account enlisting the aid of financial planners or consultants who can based on your unique situation.

Assessing Your Current Financial Situation

Compile Financial Information: Gather all of your financial information, such as bank and investment account statements, invoices and obligations.

Net worth : To determine your net worth, add up your assets (savings, investments, and real estate) and deduct your liabilities (loans and debts). This provides you with an overview of your net worth.

Analyze revenue and Expenses: Keep track of your sources of revenue and classify your monthly outgoings. You may better grasp where your money is coming from and going by doing this.

Evaluate Debt Load: Review your debts, including the interest rates and due dates, to determine your debt load. Make a strategy to handle and settle your high-interest loans first.

Evaluate Emergency reserve: Determine whether you have a reserve that can last for three to six months of living expenditures. If not, concentrate on creating one.

Analyze Your Savings and Investment Performance: Examine your savings rate and investment results. Depending on your objectives, adjust your donations.

Making a Budget: To control your monthly spending and saving, make a realistic budget. Set aside money for essentials, optional purchases, and savings objectives.

Retirement planning :Assess your retirement contributions and savings as part of your retirement planning. Depending on your preferred retirement age and way of life, modify your retirement plan.

Insurance coverage: Review your insurance coverage (health, life, and property) to make sure it satisfies your current needs.

Financial goals: Set both immediate and long-term financial objectives. These can include making a property purchase, setting aside money for college, or retiring comfortably.

Estate planning: Consider estate planning, such as wills and trusts, if necessary to protect your assets in the future.

Professional Advice: If you want specific financial advice, speak with a financial counselor.

Solutions:

Debt management: Pay off high-interest bills first to ease your financial burden.

Emergency funds: Start or increase your emergency fund to prepare for unforeseen costs.

Automation of savings: To maintain a steady stream of contributions, set up automated payments to your savings and investing accounts.

Expense reduction: Identify places where you may reduce discretionary expenditure to increase your savings.

Investment Diversification: Review your financial portfolio to make sure it is diverse and in line with your risk tolerance.

Increased Income: Look for ways to boost your income, such as taking on a second job or freelancing.

Retirement contributions :Contributions to retirement funds should be increased, if at all feasible, to ensure a comfortable retirement.

Education and skill development: Make an investment in acquiring new skills that could lead to opportunities with greater salary.

Regular checking : Checking in frequently will let you monitor your progress and make any required corrections.

Setting Clear Financial Goals.

For financial success and good money management, setting clear financial goals is crucial. Your financial decisions will have direction and purpose thanks to these goals, which will also enable you to make decisions that are in line with your long-term aims. Think about the following actions while establishing specific financial goals:

Define Your Objectives: Decide what financial goals you have first. This might involve achieving objectives like home ownership, debt repayment, retirement savings, or a dream trip.

Specify Your Objectives: Your objectives should be stated in clear, unambiguous terms. Don't just say, "save for retirement," but rather, "save a certain amount by a certain age."

Set measurable targets :Make Your Goals Measurable So That You Can Monitor Your Progress, Make Your Goals Measurable. This keeps you motivated and enables you to recognize when your objective has been reached.

Choose realistic goals: Setting ambitious objectives is fantastic, but you need also make sure they are attainable given your present financial condition. Setting too high of expectations might result in dissatisfaction and fatigue.

Establish a Timeline: Give each objective a deadline. This increases the sense of urgency and aids in resource allocation. While long-term objectives may take years to complete, short-term goals may last only a few months.

Prioritize goals: Determine the order of significance for your goals by setting them in priority. This will direct your financial choices and keep you from overextending yourself.

Break down large goals: Large goals should be broken down into smaller, more attainable steps if they are enormous. This lessens the difficulty of the task and provides you with a clear path to follow.

Quantify Your Financial Goals: Assign precise dollar amounts to your objectives. This covers both the necessary initial outlay or funds as well as recurring contributions.

Regularly examine and Adjust: Since life circumstances vary, you should periodically examine your goals and make any required adjustments. This guarantees that your objectives are still relevant and reachable.

Keep Your Discipline: Maintaining your discipline is essential to reaching your financial goals. Maintain your spending plan, actively save money, and make decisions about money that are in line with your goals.

Celebrate Milestones: Whenever you reach a key milestone or make progress, take some time to recognize your accomplishments. You may stay motivated as you go along if you receive this encouraging feedback.

Consult an Expert: If you're unclear of your financial objectives or how to reach them, consider speaking with a financial counselor. They can offer guidance that is specifically customized to your situation.

Creating a Realistic Budget.

A realistic budget requires an evaluation of your income, costs, and financial objectives. All sources of income should be listed first, followed by a breakdown of your monthly spending, including both fixed costs like rent and utilities and variable costs like food and entertainment. Be diligent and factor in sporadic costs.

Put needs before desires by budgeting money for requirements before splurging on wants. Set aside some money for savings and unexpected expenses. For a month or two, keep track of your expenditures to find any areas where you could be overspending.

Make sure your budget is balanced, covering all of your costs with entire revenue. If there is a deficit, think about reducing non-essential spending or looking for methods to boost your revenue. Review and modify your budget as needed when conditions arise.

Recall that adaptability is essential. There may be unforeseen costs, so planning for one might relieve financial strain. You may make educated decisions and strive toward a healthy financial future by making a budget that accurately represents your current financial condition and aspirations.

Understanding Your Income and Expenses.

Effective money management requires knowledge of your income and spending. What you need to know is as follows:

Track Your Revenue Sources: Make a list of all of your sources of revenue, including your salary, side jobs, investments, and other sources of income.

Categories Expense: Sort your spending into other categories, such as those for housing, transportation, food, utilities, entertainment, savings, and debt repayment.

Budgeting: Set aside money for each area of expenses in a budget. Verify that your costs do not outweigh your revenue.

Fixed vs Variable Expense: Differentiating between fixed costs (like rent or a mortgage) and variable expenses (like entertainment or eating out) will help you plan more effectively.

Emergency Funds: Set away some of your salary as an emergency fund to pay for unforeseen expenditures.

Net revenue: Subtract taxes and other deductions from your total revenue to determine your net income.

Expense Tracking tools: Use apps, spreadsheets, or financial software to keep track of your spending and income on a regular basis. You can see exactly where your money is going thanks to this.

Review often: Analyze your budget and spending patterns often. To achieve your financial objectives, adjust your budget as necessary.

Savings and investments: Set aside some of your income for savings and investments in order to achieve future objectives such as retirement, home ownership, or education.

Debt management: Pay off high-interest bills first, such credit cards, to prevent accruing interest charges that aren't essential.

Living Within Your Means: To prevent debt and financial stress, make sure your costs are constantly lower than your income.

Financial goals: Set both immediate and long-term financial objectives. These objectives should be in line with your budget.

Avoid Impulsive Spending: Consider your options before making a purchase. Allow yourself time to determine whether it is a need or a want.

Examine and Modify: Consistently examine your financial objectives and budget. Your budget should change as your life circumstances do.

Credit scores: Consider your credit score carefully. Responsible credit utilization and on-time bill payments can boost your score.

Professional Advice: If you require specialized advice based on your circumstances, speak with a financial counselor.

Remember that it takes continual work to comprehend your income and spending. You may work toward reaching your objectives and preserving your financial security by taking charge of your financial circumstances.

Chapter 2

Mastering the Art of Saving.

The ability to efficiently manage your finances to create a secure financial future is referred to as "Mastering the Art of Saving." Here are some important things to think about:

Budgeting: It's important to set and follow a budget. To find out where your money is going, keep track of your income and spending. Set aside money for savings, discretionary expenditures, and necessities.

Emergency funds: Establish an emergency fund by setting away three to six months' worth of living costs in a convenient savings account. In the event of unanticipated occurrences like sudden medical emergency or job loss, this fund serves as a safety net.

Automate Savings: Put a percentage of your paycheck into savings by using automatic transfers. The incentive to spend before saving is removed as a result.

Debt management: Pay off high-interest bills, such as credit cards, as quickly as you can. Debt reduction can free up funds for investing and saving.

Save Early: Get your savings going as soon as you can. Because of the force of compounding, money saved early has a longer growth period.

Establish Financial Goals: Specify both short- and long-term financial objectives. Having specific objectives provides you a motivation to save, whether it's for a home purchase, a trip, or a comfortable retirement.

Live Within Your Means to prevent lifestyle inflation and pointless expenditure. To have more money to save and invest, try to spend less than you make.

Invest wisely: Learn about several investing possibilities, including stocks, bonds, mutual funds, and real estate. Invest wisely. To reduce risk and increase possible earnings, diversify your assets.

Retirement planning : Contribute to retirement funds like a 401(k) or an IRA as part of your retirement planning. Use employer matches if they are offered. Your investments will have more time to develop the sooner you start.

Avoid making impulsive purchases by using mindful spending. Make a distinction between necessities and wants. Before making any large purchases, give yourself time to reflect.

Review and make adjustments: Consistently assess your financial status. As your circumstances change, alter your spending, saving, and investing plans.

Educate Yourself: Keep up your knowledge of money management, investing methods, and personal finance. You can make better selections the more you are informed.

Keep in mind that developing your saving skills involves effort and dedication. Making educated decisions and being flexible to changes in the economy and personal situations are part of a lifetime journey.

The Power of Saving: How to Start and Stay Motivated

"The Power of Saving: How to Start and Stay Motivated" focuses on the value of saving money for future objectives and financial stability. Starting your savings path and staying motivated requires:

Clear Your Goals: Decide on your savings goals, such as an emergency fund, a down payment on a home, retirement, or a trip. Focusing is made simpler by having clear objectives.

Create a budget: Make a budget and keep track of your earnings and outgoing costs to see where your money is going. A budget enables you to set aside money for savings and discover areas where you may make cuts.

Pay yourself first by considering savings as an absolute necessity. Prior to making further purchases, put some of your salary into savings.

Automatic savings: Set up automatic transfers to your savings account to automate saving. Consistency is ensured, and the urge to spend money is reduced.

Start Small: Set a modest savings goal that is doable. Increase your savings rate gradually as you become more adept at it.

Track Progress: Keep track of the expansion of your funds. Observing your development may increase motivation and strengthen positive behaviors.

Cut unnecessary expense: Reduce or eliminate unnecessary expenditure by identifying areas where you may cut back. Put that money in your savings.

Avoid Impulsive Spending: Avoid making impulsive purchases by waiting before doing so. Check to see whether it fits with your objectives.

Visualize Rewards: Consider the advantages of reaching your objectives. You can maintain focus and increase motivation by using visualization.

Keep Being Consistent: Consistency is essential. Make a commitment to save even during difficult months.

Celebrate Milestone: Celebrate important milestones and acknowledge your progress. When you hit particular saving goals, reward yourself in moderation.

Educate Yourself: Get to know various savings instruments, such as savings accounts, certificates of deposit, mutual funds, and retirement accounts. Based on your objectives, make wise selections.

Emergency fund: Build an emergency fund as a top priority to avoid having to use long-term resources to meet unforeseen costs.

Avoid Comparison: Don't draw comparisons; each person's financial journey is different. Avoid comparing your development to that of others.

Review and Modify: Consistently evaluate your financial condition and goals. Adapt your saving plan as necessary.

Seek Support: Tell others who can support you and hold you responsible about your financial objectives.

Keep in mind that saving takes time, and that there may be setbacks. Stay dedicated, make appropriate changes to your goals, and recognize your achievements. Saving money will have a significant long-term influence on your financial situation.

Choosing the Right Savings Accounts

It's important to think about things like interest rates, fees, minimum balance requirements, accessibility, and extra services like internet banking or ATM access when selecting the best savings account.

To optimize your profits, look for accounts with market-competitive interest rates. Make sure you are aware of any account-related costs, such as monthly maintenance fees or fees for using an ATM. Consider if the minimum balance requirement for the account is appropriate for your financial condition. Choose a bank account that offers simple online or mobile banking choices since accessibility is important.

Examine any extra benefits the account may offer, such as overdraft protection or linked checking accounts, before closing.

Strategies for Saving Money on Everyday Expenses

The following are some tips for cutting costs on regular expenses:

Make a budget by first keeping track of your earnings and outgoing costs. By doing so, you'll be able to see where your money is going and find places where you may make savings.

Cook at Home: Making meals at home is usually more affordable than going out to eat. Additionally, you have more control over the components and serving sizes.

Utilize Coupons and Discounts: Before making purchases, both online and offline, check for coupons, promo codes, and discounts.

Buying in bulk may usually result in long-term financial savings, particularly for non-perishable goods that you use regularly.

Comparison shop to make sure you're getting the greatest bargain. Before making a purchase, check costs at other stores or online merchants.

Limit impulsive purchases and abstain from making them. Before making a non-essential purchase, give yourself some time to consider it.

Reduce Subscription Services: Review your subscriptions and think about discontinuing those that you don't use regularly.

Reduce Utility Use: Use less water and electricity to cut costs. Use energy-efficient appliances, disconnect gadgets, and turn off the lights.

Use Public Transportation: If at all feasible, take the bus or carpool to save money on gas and parking.

DIY and Repairs: Learn how to perform simple maintenance and repair jobs on your own rather than engaging a professional.

Cancel Unused subscriptions: You may save money by terminating any subscriptions you don't use, including those for streaming services, gyms, and other things.

Shop Second hand: Consider buying second hand gadgets, furniture, and apparel to save money in comparison to brand-new products.

Plan Shopping list : Make a list of what you need to buy before you go to the store to prevent impulse purchases.

Automate Savings: To make sure you're continuously putting money aside, set up automated transfers from your checking account to your savings account.

Negotiate bills: Reduced costs for internet, cable, and other services can be negotiated by contacting your service providers.

Avoid Brand Loyalty by choosing generic or store-brand goods instead, which are frequently less expensive and of equivalent quality.

Track Expenses : Use applications or spreadsheets to keep track of your costs. By doing so, you may maintain accountability and find room for development.

Limit Eating Out: Cut back on the number of times you eat out or order takeout. Over time, it can result in large savings.

Utilize Cash Back Rewards: If you have credit cards that provide cash back rewards, use them wisely to accrue points for purchases.

Plan ahead: To minimize financial stress at the last minute, anticipate major costs, such as vacations or special occasions, and lay money away in advance.

Keep in mind that even tiny adjustments to your spending patterns over time might add up. It involves making deliberate decisions and identifying places where wasteful spending may be reduced.

Emergency Funds: Your Safety Net in Tough Times

A quantity of money saved aside as an emergency reserve can be used to meet unforeseen costs or other financial difficulties, acting as a safety net in trying times. What you need to know is as follows:

Purpose of an Emergency fund: The goal of an emergency fund is to prevent you from using credit cards, loans, or all of your assets to cover unforeseen costs like medical bills, auto repairs, or a sudden loss of employment.

Ideal Amount: Three to six months' worth of living costs should be saved in your emergency fund, according to several financial experts. Depending on your unique situation, such as employment security, family size, and monthly spending, this amount may change.

Accessibility: Place your emergency fund in a liquid, quickly accessible account, such as a money market or normal savings account. This makes sure you can immediately access the money when you need it.

Regular Contributions: Set aside a percentage of your monthly paycheck to develop your emergency fund. It should be treated as a non-negotiable cost, similar to paying bills.

Prioritize High-Interest Debt: To save money on interest payments, think about paying off high-interest debts (such credit cards) before concentrating only on your emergency fund.

Distinct from Other Savings: You should keep your emergency fund distinct from other savings objectives, such as trips or home purchases. By doing this, you can keep the fund out of non-emergency situations.

Review and Replenish: Reevaluate your emergency fund on a regular basis to take into account changes in your financial condition. If you withdraw money from it, make it a point to reload it as soon as you can.

Adjust for Life events: The amount of your emergency fund may need to be adjusted in response to significant life events, including a new job or the expansion of your family.

Peace of Mind: Having a sizable emergency fund gives you peace of mind, lowering your stress levels during trying times and giving you a feeling of financial stability.

Insurance Coverage: In addition to having an emergency fund, you should make sure you have enough health, vehicle, and house insurance coverage to reduce financial risks.

Keep in mind that having an emergency fund is about being ready for anything. It's an essential part of your entire financial plan and offers stability in difficult circumstances.

Chapter 3

The Road to Debt Freedom

"The phrase "Road to Debt Freedom" describes the path and methods people take to pay off their debts and become financially independent. Here are some crucial actions and ideas to remember along the way:

Evaluation: To start, make a list of every debt you have, including credit card debt, loans, and other financial responsibilities. Take note of the interest rates, required minimum payments, and total balances owing.

Budgeting: Lay out your monthly income and spending in a thorough budget. Spend as much as you can on debt reduction while still paying for basic expenses.

Select a debt payback plan, such as the debt snowball or debt avalanche. The debt snowball provides psychological gains by emphasizing paying off the smaller obligations first. To reduce interest payments, the debt avalanche prioritizes obligations with higher interest rates first.

Create an emergency fund with three to six months' worth of living costs. By doing this, you can prevent debt accumulation when unplanned costs emerge.

Spend Less: Reduce discretionary spending and use the savings toward paying off debt. This can entail cutting out on entertainment, dining out, or unnecessary buying.

Increase income: In order to increase your income, look for other employment options like side gigs or freelancing. Use this extra money to pay down your debt.

Negotiate Interest Rates: Speak with your creditors to work out a better deal. Most of your payment will go toward lowering the principal debt if the rate is lower.

Consider refinancing or consolidating your debts to get a loan with a cheaper interest rate if you have several loans that you need to pay off. Refinancing can also assist in lowering interest costs.

Credit counseling: If paying off your bills is too difficult, consider using credit counseling services. They can assist you in drafting a detailed repayment strategy.

Be Disciplined: Adhere to your spending plan and debt-repayment strategy. During this time, refrain from taking on any new debt.

Celebrate Milestones: Recognize and rejoice for each loan that has been paid off. You remain inspired and driven as a result.

Financial Education: Gain knowledge of investing, managing money, and personal finance. You may avoid future debt by making educated decisions thanks to this knowledge.

Long-Term Planning: After being debt-free, keep up your strict financial management routine. Plan, invest, and save for future objectives.

Keep in mind that getting out of debt takes time, dedication, and consistency. You get closer to obtaining financial security and independence with each step you take. Even though the procedure could be lengthy, the benefits are well worth the time and work.

Types of Debt: Good vs. Bad

Based on elements like interest rates, payback conditions, and the reason for borrowing, debt may be divided into many forms. An overview of debt categories, highlighting good and bad debt, is provided below, along with various solutions:

Debt categories:

Mortgage Debt: A mortgage is a loan used to buy a property. Generally speaking, it is viewed as a long-term investment.

Student loans: Credit taken out to pay for schooling. Excessive student loan debt can be burdensome even though it might result in greater employment possibilities.

Loans for autos: Used to purchase a car. In general, if the automobile is required for employment or other important activities, they are seen as reasonable.

Debt from credit cards: Taking out loans against a credit line. If not handled appropriately, high interest rates can make this kind of debt risky.

Personal loans: Unsecured borrowing for a range of needs. These can be prudently utilized for investments or emergencies, but going beyond can cause issues.

Payday loans: Very expensive, short-term loans that must be returned with the next salary. They should be avoided since they frequently charge high prices.

Bad vs. Good Debt

Debt that has the potential to raise your net worth or prospective earnings in the future is referred to as **good debt**. Getting a mortgage for a house or taking out student loans for schooling are two examples.

Bad debt is debt that doesn't advance your finances and is frequently racked up for luxuries. Payday loans and credit card debt with high interest rates are two examples.

Solutions:

Budgeting: To efficiently manage your funds, make a budget. Set aside money for debt repayment and follow your strategy.

Build an emergency fund to take care of unforeseen costs, minimizing the need for credit cards or loans.

Prioritize High-Interest Debt: To prevent accruing excessive interest fees, concentrate on paying off high-interest debt first.

Consolidation: Take into account combining multiple loans with differing interest rates to pay off high-interest obligations. This may ease the burden of repaying.

Choose a debt payback plan that works for you from the two options, debt snowball and debt avalanche. The debt avalanche technique concentrates on loans with the highest interest rates, whereas the debt snowball method prioritizes paying off lesser bills first.

Seek Professional Assistance: If you're having trouble managing your finances, think about enrolling in credit counseling or debt management programs.

To effectively manage your debt, bear in mind that you must make intelligent choices and have a long-term view of your financial situation.

Creating a Debt Repayment Plan

There are various phases involved in creating a debt payback plan:

Information gathering: Compile all the data you can on your debts, such as the amounts, interest rates, required minimum payments, and due dates.

Make a list of your debts and prioritize them based on the interest rate or total amount owed. You can then concentrate on loans with high interest rates.

Access your finance : Determine how much you can set aside for debt repayment by assessing your monthly income and spending.

Create a budget that covers your necessary costs and leaves room to pay off debt. Spend less on non-essentials to generate more funds for debt repayment.

If you can, try to negotiate better terms or lower interest rates with your creditors. This may assist in lowering the total cost of your loan.

Select a Repayment Plan: There are two well-liked tactics namely:

- **Avalanche Method**: Reduce total interest paid by paying off loans with the highest interest rates first.

- Pay off bills with the lowest sums first for immediate gains, then move on to debts with higher balances, using the **snowball method.**

Payment Allocation: Distribute your resources in accordance with your selected approach. Pay the minimal amount due on all bills while allocating additional money to your highest priority obligation.

Follow the Plan: Maintain a rigorous and regular payback schedule. If you can, automate your payments to prevent missing deadlines.

Track Progress: Keep yourself motivated by keeping track of your advancement and revising your strategy as necessary. It might be reassuring to see your debt balance go down.

Observe Milestones: As you pay off each obligation, take time to recognize your accomplishments. You may find it easier to keep motivated if you do this.

Avoid Taking on New Debt: To avoid ruining your work while paying off existing debt, avoid taking up new debt.

Consider creating a modest emergency fund to pay for unforeseen costs so you won't have to rely on credit cards in difficult times.

Professional Assistance: If your debt situation is unmanageable, think about getting assistance from financial planners or credit counseling organizations.

Keep in mind that developing a repayment strategy takes commitment and perseverance. It's a methodical procedure that will ultimately result in debt freedom.

Negotiating with Creditors and Managing Debt Collectors

Effective communication and money management are required while negotiating with creditors and with debt collectors. Here is a quick summary:

Communication: As soon as you suspect difficulties, get in touch with your creditors. Clearly describe your circumstances and go over possible alternatives, such as lower interest rates or altered payment schedules.

Recognize your rights: Learn about the rules that protect you against harassment and abusive debt collection methods, such as the Fair Debt Collection methods Act (FDCPA) in the U.S.

Debt validation: If a debt collector contacts you, ask for a written debt validation to make sure the information is accurate and legitimate.

Debt negotiation: Offer a workable repayment plan that fits your financial condition when dealing with creditors or collectors. They could be OK with a one-time payment or a reduced amount.

Documentation: Maintain copies of all correspondence, contracts, and payments. This can be useful if any future issues occur.

Remain arranged: To organize your funds and set debt repayment priorities, create a budget. Spend your money prudently to prevent late payments.

Avoid using forceful techniques; when interacting with collectors, maintain composure. Stay away from confrontational situations and pressure.

Consolidation and settlement: If your debt load is high, look into possibilities like debt consolidation loans or debt settlement programs. These might make it easier for you to handle several bills.

Professional assistance: If talks get too difficult, think about contacting credit counseling organizations or debt management-focused attorneys.

Protect your credit score: Ensure that your payments are made on time and that you are handling your money wisely to protect your credit score.

Remember that when dealing with creditors and debt collectors, transparency and initiative are essential.

Avoiding Common Debt Traps

It's essential to stay out of frequent debt pitfalls to retain financial stability. Here are some essential pointers to assist you avoid debt pitfalls:

Budgeting: To keep track of your income and spending, make a monthly budget. You may better manage your finances and avoid overspending if you do this.

Create an emergency fund to pay for unforeseen bills. Having this cushion might help you avoid having to use your credit card or borrow money during an emergency.

Live Within Your Means: Resist the urge to spend excessively on items you cannot afford. Put needs before desires and budget your money carefully.

Credit Cards: Be careful while using credit cards. To avoid paying excessive interest rates, pay off your debt in full each month. Keep your balance low so it doesn't accrue interest.

Interest Rates: Be mindful of the loan and credit card interest rates. Debts with high interest rates can quickly mount up and be challenging to manage.

Debt to Income Ratio: Be mindful of your debt to income ratio. A high ratio shows that your debt to income ratio is out of line.

Avoid Payday Loans: Avoid taking out payday loans or other short-term, high-interest loans. These loans have exceptionally high interest rates, which can cause a debt cycle.

Comparison Shopping : Before making a large purchase, do your homework and compare pricing. This might assist you in locating the greatest offers and preventing needless debt.

Negotiate conditions: When taking out loans, bargain with lenders to ensure that the conditions, interest rates, and repayment terms are manageable for you.

Track Your Debt: Keep a list of your debts, together with their interest rates and due dates. This will enable you to maintain organization and send payments on schedule.

Financial Education: Make the time to learn about managing your money and personal finances. The better prepared you are to avoid financial traps, the more you will comprehend.

Avoid Making Impulse Purchases: Think twice before buying something to be sure you actually need it. Impulsive purchases may result in debt and regret.

Carefully Consolidate Debt: While consolidating debt might be beneficial, do your homework and pick reliable businesses. A secured loan, such as a home equity loan, should not be used to consolidate unsecured debt.

Savings Goals: Set financial objectives and strive toward them. This may inspire you to cut back on needless spending and give you a feeling of direction.

Never Cosign: Before agreeing to sign someone else's debt, give it some thought. You'll be liable if the other party doesn't make payments, which might result in financial issues.

Keep in mind that avoiding debt traps involves self-control, restraint, and a dedication to ethical money management. If you already have debt, you should get expert guidance to create a strategy for managing and repaying it.

Chapter 4

Investing for the Future

Allocating your funds with the intention of earning returns over time is part of investing for the future. Here are some important things to think about:

Establish your financial objectives and evaluate your risk tolerance: Your investing plan will be determined by a number of variables, including your time frame, goals, and level of tolerance with any swings in the value of your investments.

Diversification: Spread your assets among several asset classes (stocks, bonds, real estate, etc.) to diversify your portfolio and lower your risk. If one investment does poorly, diversification helps reduce losses.

Long-Term View: Over the long term, investing is typically most successful. Your assets may increase dramatically over time thanks to compounding returns.

Start Early: Your money has more time to grow the sooner you start investing. Over many years, even modest, ongoing contributions can have a significant impact.

Types of Investments:

Stocks: Purchasing ownership stakes in a business. Due to market volatility, they come with a higher risk but also the potential for huge gains.

Bonds: Loans given to organizations or governments in return for interest payments. Though often thought to carry less risk than stocks, they may also provide lesser returns.

Mutual Funds/ETFs: Groups of investors' funds used to purchase a diverse portfolio. They offer immediate diversity.

Real estate: Purchasing a home for future capital growth or rental revenue. can provide a combination of income and room for development.

Retirement Accounts: For long-term savings, accounts like 401(k)s or IRAs provide tax advantages.

Do some research and educate yourself on the investments you're thinking about. Know the potential for development of the businesses or assets you are investing in.

Charges: Keep in mind that over time, investment charges including fees and expenditures may reduce your profits.

Rebalance: Regularly assess and modify your portfolio to make sure it is in line with your objectives. Your ideal asset allocation may change as time goes on due to changes in the value of various investments.

Avoid Making Emotional Decisions: Don't let quick market changes influence your choices. Poor decisions might result from emotional emotions.

Professional Advice: To assist in developing a strategy specific to your position and goals, think about speaking with a financial counselor.

Keep in mind that investing entails risks and that there is no surefire method to forecast how assets will perform in the future. It's crucial to have patience, be knowledgeable, and set realistic goals.

Introduction to Investing: Demystifying the Basics.

A solid grasp of the financial world is what students will get through the course "Introduction to Investing: Demystifying the Basics". It goes through fundamental ideas and methods like:

Investment Types: Highlights the features, possible hazards, and benefits of several investment alternatives, including stocks, bonds, mutual funds, ETFs, and real estate.

Risk and Return: Explains the connection between prospective risks and rewards. Investors must strike the correct balance for their level of risk tolerance because larger profits frequently come with higher hazards.

Diversification: Stresses the value of distributing assets across several asset classes in order to lower risk. Diversification lessens the effects of substandard performance in a single area.

Time Horizon : Discusses the relevance of an investor's time horizon when holding an investment. Higher potential profits and a stronger capacity to withstand market swings may frequently be achieved with longer time horizons.

Market Analysis: Introduces fundamental and technical analysis as well as other key techniques for studying the financial markets. These methods aid in the decision-making process for investors.

Investment Strategies: Discusses many investment strategies, each with its own strategy and goals, such as value investing, growth investing, and income investing.

Investment Vehicles: Describes brokerage accounts, taxable accounts, and retirement accounts (such as IRAs), as well as the advantages and tax ramifications of each.

Costs and Fees: Emphasizes the effect that fees, commissions, and charges have on the returns on investments. In the long term, cheaper solutions could be better.

Market indexes: Explains the meaning of prominent market indexes like the S&P 500 and Dow Jones Industrial Average and introduces them.

Behavioral finance: Discusses frequent problems and how psychological biases can influence financial decisions.

Long-Term Perspective: Emphasizes the value of a methodical, patient approach to investing while avoiding emotional responses to transient market changes.

Inflation and taxes: Discusses how inflation and taxes might eventually reduce investment profits and offers solutions to lessen their effects.

The goal of the course is to arm novices with the information they need to make wise investment choices that are in line with their financial objectives and risk tolerance. Though the course gives you a good basis, effective investing requires constant learning and adjusting to market fluctuations.

Building Your Investment Portfolio

Planning and thought go into creating an investing portfolio. To remember, have the following in mind:

Investment Objectives: Specify your financial goals. Are you putting money aside to increase your wealth, for a down payment on a home, or for retirement? Your investing plan will be shaped by your ambitions.

Recognize your level of risk tolerance. While some investments are more reliable but with lower potential returns, others are riskier but with larger potential returns. Based on how much risk you can tolerate, balance your investment portfolio.

Diversification: Avoid putting all of your eggs in one basket by diversifying. To lower overall risk, diversify your portfolio among several asset types (stocks, bonds, real estate, etc.).

Asset Allocation: Determine how much of your portfolio will be allocated to each asset class in your asset allocation strategy. Your objectives, risk tolerance, and time horizon all play a role in this.

Research investments carefully before making a decision. Know the business, sector, or fund you are investing in. Important indicators include past results and potential outcomes.

Perspective over the Long Run: Investing is a long-term project. Steer clear of forming snap judgments based on momentary market changes.

Be mindful of the costs and fees related to investing in products. Over time, high costs might gradually reduce your earnings.

Tax Efficiency: Think about how your investments will affect your taxes. You may keep more of your earnings by using tax-efficient measures.

Regular Review: Check to see if your portfolio is still in line with your objectives on a regular basis. If required, rebalance to keep your desired asset allocation.

Establish an emergency fund with 3-6 months' worth of expenditures before investing. This will assist you in avoiding selling investments during difficult times.

Investment vehicles: Pick the right ones, such as individual stocks, bonds, mutual funds, exchange-traded funds (ETFs), and more. Each has unique qualities and advantages.

Stay Informed :Keep up with financial news and trends to stay informed. On the other hand, refrain from making snap judgments based on recent events.

Professional Advice: If you're new to investing or have complicated financial circumstances, you should think about seeing a financial counselor.

Have patience: Investment growth might be slow. Defy the urge to seek rapid rewards.

Behavioral Control: Poor investing outcomes might result from emotional decisions. Adhere to your plan and refrain from acting under the influence of greed or fear.

Do not forget that creating an investing portfolio is an ongoing effort. It necessitates continuous learning and adaptation in response to modifications in your life, the economy, and the financial markets.

Diving into Stocks, Bonds, and Mutual Funds.

Understanding various investment kinds and how they function is necessary before diving into stocks, bonds, and mutual funds. Here is a quick summary:

Stocks:

Stocks signify ownership in a corporation. Purchasing stocks makes you a shareholder and gives you ownership of a piece of the business.
A company's performance, market sentiment, and industry trends are just a few examples of the variables that can cause stock values to fluctuate.
High return potential, but more risk in comparison to other investments.

Bonds:

Bonds are debt instruments that are issued by firms or governments to raise money. In essence, when you purchase a bond you are giving the issuer money in return for periodic interest payments and the repayment of the principle amount upon maturity.

Though possibly offering smaller returns, they are typically thought to be less hazardous than equities.

Mutual Funds:

Mutual funds aggregate the capital of many investors and use it to buy a variety of stocks, bonds, and other assets.

Since they are handled by qualified fund managers, they may be an excellent choice for novice investors who want a hands-off approach to investing.

provides diversification by distributing risk across several assets.

Important information

Risk and Return :Stocks offer a larger potential return but a higher potential risk than other investments. Bonds provide greater stability, but often give lesser yields. Mutual funds offer a well-rounded strategy.

Diversification: Spreading investments across several assets can help control risk through diversification. Due to their diversified holdings, mutual funds inherently offer diversification.

Research the firms, ETFs, or bonds you are interested in purchasing before making an investment. Recognize their managerial style, track record of performance, and overall financial standing.

Investment Horizon: Think about how long you want to invest. Bonds provide stability for short-term objectives, while stocks may be more suited for long-term gain.

Costs: Management fees are charged for some bonds and mutual funds. Transaction charges may apply to stocks. The impact of these costs on your returns should be considered.

Market Trends: Keep abreast of global events, economic data, and market trends that may have an impact on your investments.

Risk Tolerance: Recognize your investing objectives and risk tolerance. Your investing decisions will be influenced by your capacity to withstand market changes.

Always remember to get advice from financial experts or professionals before making any investing decisions. They can give you tailored guidance based on your financial objectives and condition.

Exploring Retirement Accounts and Investment Vehicles.

It's essential to investigate retirement plans and investing options if you want to safeguard your financial future. Basics are as follows:

Accounts for Retirement:

Employer-sponsored plan called a 401(k) where you can contribute a percentage of your salary and frequently receive a corporate match.

Individual plan with tax-deferred contributions known as a traditional IRA; taxes are due upon retirement withdrawal.

Individual retirement account (IRA) that allows for after-tax contributions and tax-free withdrawals in retirement.
Investment Instruments:

Stocks are ownership stakes in a corporation; they carry a higher risk and possible reward.

Bonds are debt instruments that are issued by firms or governments; they typically have a lesser risk than equities but also have a smaller potential return.

Mutual funds: Invests in diverse portfolios of stocks, bonds, or other assets by pooling the funds of several investors.

Exchange-Traded Funds (ETFs) offer diversification and minimal costs; they are similar to mutual funds but traded on stock exchanges.

Real estate: Purchasing homes with the intention of renting them out or selling them for a profit.

Index Funds: Passive investment vehicles that closely follow a particular market index in an effort to match its performance.

Insurance agreements known as annuities that offer recurring payouts in return for a one-time payment.
Considerations:

Risk Tolerance: Determine how ready you are to put up with market turbulence.

Diversification: Spreading assets across a variety of asset types can help to lower risk.

Time horizon: Your investing time horizon, which determines your risk appetite and approach.

Management fees, spending ratios, and other charges should be considered because they can affect results.

Tax Implications: The tax treatment of contributions and withdrawals from various accounts varies.
Pension Planning:

Start Early: Early investment is very advantageous due to the power of compounding.

Set Goals: Determine your retirement needs and the lifestyle you wish to lead before setting goals.

Regular Investments: Making consistent investments over time will help you accumulate money.

Review and Modify: Regularly reevaluate your investments and modify your approach as necessary.

Financial Advisor: For individualized help, see a qualified financial planner.

Investment Research: Research your possibilities for investments and learn about various investing techniques.

Remember that careful thought, diverse assets, and a long-term outlook are the keys to effective retirement planning. It's crucial to adjust your strategy to fit your unique needs and objectives.

Chapter 5

Navigating Major Financial Decisions

Making sense of important financial choices is essential for safeguarding your financial future. What you need to know is as follows:

Establish definite financial goals. To start, decide what your short- and long-term financial goals are. Clear objectives give focus, whether they be for paying off debt, purchasing a home, or investing for retirement.

Budgeting: Lay down your income and spending in a thorough budget. By doing so, you'll be able to see where your money is going and find places where you may cut costs.

Emergency fund: Build a reserve of at least three to six months' worth of living expenditures for emergencies. This serves as a backup plan in case of unforeseen financial problems.

Debt management: Pay off high-interest debt first, such as credit cards. To attack debts methodically, use techniques like the debt snowball or avalanche method.

Investment Knowledge: Gain an understanding of the many types of investments (stocks, bonds, real estate, etc.) and how they correspond to your financial objectives and risk tolerance. To better minimize risk, think about diversifying your investing portfolio.

Retirement planning: Get a head start on saving. Utilize 401(k) and other employer-sponsored retirement programs, and educate yourself about IRAs.

Insurance: Examine your insurance requirements, including those for health, life, house, and vehicle insurance. Make sure you have enough coverage to guard against unforeseen circumstances.

Tax Planning: Recognize how taxes affect your financial situation. Investigate tax-efficient investing methods and utilize tax credits and deductions.

Estate planning: Create or alter your will, name beneficiaries, and, if necessary, take into consideration creating trusts as part of estate planning. This guarantees that your assets are allocated in line with your intentions.

Professional Advice: When required, seek the advice of accountants, financial consultants, or estate planners. They can offer professional advice catered to your particular set of circumstances.

Continuous Learning should never stop since the financial world is always changing. Aside from credible financial websites and books, there are other excellent resources.

Risk management involves identifying and reducing financial hazards by diversifying investments and having proper insurance coverage. Avoid making hasty judgments motivated by greed or fear.

Avoid lifestyle inflation by resisting the need to substantially raise your spending when your income rises. Instead, put more money aside for investments and savings.

Assess and Modify: Consistently assess your financial plan to make sure it reflects your evolving objectives and situation. To keep on course, adjust as necessary.

Maintain Your Discipline and Patience: Reaching Financial Goals Requires Time and Discipline. During market turbulence, exercise patience, adhere to your strategy, and refrain from making snap judgments.

Keep in mind that making financial decisions is an ongoing process. To make decisions that are in accordance with your financial goals, it's critical to be informed, practice discipline, and seek expert advice as needed.

Buying a Home: From Renting to Owning

Purchasing a home is a big financial decision that requires a lot of work and thought. Here is a thorough guide on going from renting to buying a house:

Examine your finances:Examine your existing financial condition, taking into account your earnings, spending, and savings.
Determine how much you can afford to spend on a down payment, a monthly mortgage, and other expenses associated with homeownership.

Increase Your Credit:Keep your credit score high since it has an impact on your ability to obtain a mortgage with favorable conditions.

Invest in Down Payments:To avoid paying private mortgage insurance (PMI), aim for a down payment of at least 20% of the home's cost.

Create a Budget: Set a budget for a home, taking into account not just the purchase price but also the expenditures of upkeep, insurance, and property taxes.

Get a Mortgage Pre-Approval: Get pre-approved for a mortgage loan by contacting lenders. This makes you a more appealing purchase and helps you understand your financing capabilities.

Search for a Real Estate Agent: Work with a real estate professional who has the necessary skills to guide you through the home-buying process.

Look for Homes: Start looking for a home while keeping location, size, amenities, and resale value in mind.

Negotiate and Present a Proposal: Make a buyer an offer as soon as you locate a house that meets your needs. Be ready to bargain as necessary.

Home appraisal and inspection: To confirm the property's condition and worth once an offer is accepted, schedule a home inspection and appraisal.

Dependable financing: Complete your mortgage loan, including giving the lender the required paperwork and information.

Closing expenses: Be ready for closing charges, which may include loan fees, title search fees, insurance premiums, and other expenses.

Final Day: Receive the keys to your new house after signing the required documents and paying the closing charges.

Arrive and Set Up Shop: Plan your relocation, switch utilities, and complete any repairs or house upgrades that are required.

Homeownership obligations: Recognize your obligations as a homeowner, such as those related to property upkeep, insurance, and taxes.

Plan a budget for ongoing costs: Continue setting aside money in your budget for your mortgage, utilities, maintenance, and unforeseen repairs.

Create Home Equity: As you make mortgage payments over time, you'll increase your home's equity, which may be a valuable asset.

Organize Your Future: Think about your long-term objectives and how owning a home fits into your financial strategy.

Keep in mind that property ownership has both financial and upkeep obligations. Throughout the process, it's critical to be financially prepared and make wise choices. Making a smooth transition from renting to house ownership may be achieved by seeking the advice of a financial expert and conducting extensive study.

Making Smart Vehicle Choices: Buying, Leasing, and Beyond

Buying, leasing, and other factors, as well as others, must all be taken into account when choosing a smart car. What you need to know is as follows:

Define Your Needs: Begin by being aware of your requirements. Budget, daily commute, cargo space, and the number of passengers are a few things to think about. Establish whether a vehicle, SUV, truck, or something else is required.

Budget: Set a realistic budget that accounts for recurring expenses like insurance, gasoline, maintenance, and taxes in addition to the purchase or lease price.

New vs Old: Consider if you want a new or used car before making your choice. Used automobiles are less expensive but may have a shorter lifespan than new cars, which often carry warranties and the newest amenities.

Research: Examine several brands and models that meet your requirements. Check out the safety features, dependability ratings, and reviews.

Websites and forums are useful sources for user reviews.

Think About Fuel economy: If you have a long commute, consider fuel economy. Over time, fuel savings from hybrid, electric, or fuel-efficient cars are possible.

Safety: Prioritize safety features including lane-keeping and adaptive cruise control as well as airbags, anti-lock brakes, stability control, and other advanced driver assistance systems (ADAS).

Test Drive: Before making a choice, always take a car for a test drive. This enables you to evaluate handling, comfort, and any possible problems.

Calculate the total cost of ownership during the lifespan of the car, taking into account depreciation, insurance, maintenance, and fuel expenditures.

Consider financing alternatives, such as loans or cash purchases, if you want to buy. Understand the lease's conditions, mileage restrictions, and potential fines if you're leasing.

Resale value: Take into account the car's resale value. Your long-term expenditures may be impacted by the brands and models that retain their worth the best.

Negotiate: Whether you are purchasing or leasing, bargain the price. Often, there is potential for negotiating with dealerships, so be prepared to barter.

Insurance: Obtain insurance estimates for the automobiles you are thinking about purchasing. Based on the make and model, insurance prices might vary greatly.

Ownership vs Leasing: Be aware of the distinctions between ownership and leasing. Ownership entails complete control as well as whole accountability for upkeep. While leasing may provide reduced monthly payments, it also has restrictions and mileage caps.

Maintenance: For your car to last a long time, regular maintenance is essential. Budgeting should take maintenance expenditures into account.

Warranties: Review the manufacturer's warranty for further information. Even though the terms and coverage may differ, it can provide you peace of mind for unforeseen repairs.

Worth at Resale: Some models and brands keep their worth better over time. If you intend to sell or trade in your car in the future, take this into account.

Consider Other Options: Investigate other options, such as public transportation, ride-sharing, or car-sharing, which may be more affordable for some.

Environmental Impact: If the environment is important to you, look into green solutions like hybrid or electric cars.

Think about your long-term objectives. Are you seeking a temporary fix or do you want to retain the car for a long time?

Legal Considerations: Become familiar with your local legislation, pollution standards, and any applicable incentives or rebates for electric or hybrid vehicles.

Always keep in mind that selecting a smart car requires balancing your unique requirements, financial constraints, and personal preferences. Do careful study, take your time, and don't make a choice too quickly.

Marriage, Family, and Money: Combining Financial Lives

The success of a marriage, family, and financial relationship depends on careful thought and open communication in all three areas of life. What you should know about them, including how to combine your financial life, is as follows:

Marriage:

Marriage is an emotional and legal bond between two individuals. It represents a relationship based on adoration, trust, and respect for one another.

Communication: It's important to be honest and open with one another. Talk about your marriage's duties and responsibilities as well as your beliefs, objectives, and expectations.

Legal Aspects: Be aware of how marriage will affect your legal rights, taxes, and inheritance.
Family:

Building of family

Choosing to Have Children: If you decide to have children, make plans for their upbringing, education, and general well-being.

Support system: Family members may be a helpful support system. Keep in touch with both yourself and your spouse's families.

Roles and responsibilities: Clearly identify duties and responsibilities within the family while taking into account the preferences and strengths of both partners.

Money:

Understand each other's financial attitudes, routines, and objectives to ensure financial compatibility. Are you a spender or a saver? Do you owe money? Which financial priorities do you have?

Budgeting: Establish a shared budget that details your income, spending, and savings objectives. Review it often and make any adjustments.

Create an emergency fund to pay for unforeseen bills. Aim for three to six months' worth of spending.

Debt management: Talk about your current debts and how you want to handle and settle them together.

Investment: Select investing options to ensure your long-term financial stability. Think about varying your investing portfolio.

Retirement Planning: Make a joint retirement plan. Think about pensions, retirement funds, and other investing possibilities.

Adding Financial Lives Together:

Joint or separate accounts: Determine whether to keep separate accounts, establish joint accounts, or utilize a combination of the two. Your tastes and the state of your finances will determine this.

Transparency: Describe your financial condition openly. Share your partner's income, spending, and account information.

Financial Goals: Set common financial objectives like purchasing a home, putting money down for college, or retiring. Adapt your spending and saving practices to these objectives.

Discuss your emergency plan in case there is a situation when there is a loss of income, a disability, or unplanned bills.

Seek Professional Advice: If you need assistance navigating difficult financial decisions, speak with a financial professional or counselor.

It's important to keep in mind that integrating your financial life into your marriage is a big step, so it's crucial to strike a balance that benefits both of you. You may create a solid and enduring connection by maintaining open lines of communication and sharing a commitment to financial security.

Chapter 6

Achieving Financial Growth

The objective of achieving financial development is complex and requires a variety of tactics and ideas. The following essential ideas can assist you in comprehending and pursuing financial growth:

Financial goals: Establish definite, attainable financial objectives. These can include beginning a company, buying a home, paying off debt, or investing for retirement.

Budget: Making a budget will help you keep track of your income and spending. This assists you in figuring out where your money is going and locating opportunities for saving or investing.

Establish an emergency fund to pay for unforeseen costs through saving. Save enough money to cover your living expenses for three to six months.

Manage your debt by paying off high-interest obligations as soon as you can. Payoff of high-interest loans and credit card debt should come first.

Investing: Take into account putting your resources into securities like stocks, bonds, properties, or mutual funds. To spread risk, diversify your investments.

Compounded Interest: Be aware of its influence. As you receive interest on both your initial investment and the cumulative interest, your investments might increase enormously over time.

Risk Tolerance: Evaluate your degree of comfort with risk and build an investing strategy accordingly. Younger investors may often accept greater risk in exchange for possibly larger profits.

Financial Education: Continue to educate yourself about investing opportunities and personal finance. Keep up with the latest business and economic news.

Professional Advice: To receive individualized advice on your financial strategy, speak with financial counselors or specialists.

Focus on growing your income by advancing your career, taking on side jobs, or starting your own business.

Tax Efficiency: Use tax-advantaged funds like 401(k)s and IRAs to maximize your tax strategy. Recognize the tax benefits and deductions that are available to you.

Long-Term Perspective: When making financial decisions, keep the long term in mind. Avoid making hasty financial decisions based on transient market swings.

Lifestyle Decisions: Think about how your lifestyle decisions affect your ability to build your money. Spending excessively on non-essentials should be avoided.

Planning ahead for emergencies such as sickness or job loss involves having insurance and a backup plan in place.

Review and Adjust: Regularly assess your financial plan and make any adjustments in light of any modifications to your objectives, priorities, or surroundings.

Patience and discipline are frequently required to achieve financial progress. When faced with obstacles or failures, stay committed to your plan.

Network and Relationship: Develop a solid professional network and keep positive financial ties with lenders, creditors, and advisers.

Legacy planning: Consider how you want to use estate planning to leave a financial legacy for future generations.

Keep in mind that financial development is a process that takes time and that there are no surefire fast cuts. Knowledge, discipline, and a well-thought-out plan are all necessary. To safeguard your financial future, start small, establish attainable objectives, and constantly work toward them.

Side Hustles and Additional Income Streams

You can make money outside of your main work or source of income by engaging in side jobs and other sources of revenue. What you need to know is as follows:

Definition:

A side hustle is defined as a part-time career, endeavor, or business that you pursue outside of your normal work or major source of income. It's frequently explored as a way to supplement your income or to follow a hobby.

Reasons to Work a Side Job

Financial stability: Additional income might act as a safety net for unforeseen costs.

Debt reduction: It can facilitate quicker debt repayment.
Financial Goals: Put money aside for a particular purpose, such as a trip or retirement.

Skills development: Side businesses can help you develop your skills and expertise.

Passion Projects: Go after passions or pastimes that can also bring in money.

Forms of side businesses:

Offering services such as writing, graphic design, or web development on a freelance basis.

E-commerce is the practice of selling goods online using sites like Etsy or Amazon.

Consulting: Offering your subject-matter knowledge.
Driving for services like Uber or delivering meals are examples of ridesharing or delivery.

Create online content through podcasting, blogging, or YouTube.

Investing: Dividends, stocks, or real estate investing.

Effective time management is necessary to juggle a side gig and your primary work. Regarding the amount of time you can devote, be reasonable.

Legal and Tax Considerations: Recognize how your side business may affect your taxes, company licenses, and permits.

Market research includes examining the competition and the level of demand for your goods or services.

Financial management: Keep a record of your side-hustle-related earnings and outlays. Set money aside for taxes.

Networking might help you locate possibilities and clients for your side business.

Skill development: Investment in developing your abilities can help you succeed in your side business.

Burnout Prevention: Avoid overextending yourself to avoid burnout. Burnout may be avoided by maintaining balance.

Scaling: If your side business succeeds, think about how to expand it.

Long-Term Goals: Consider the relationship between your side business and your long-term financial and professional objectives.

Risk management: Recognize the dangers posed by your side business and take the necessary safeguards.

Passion and Persistence: Pick a side business you are enthusiastic about since it will help you stay motivated when things become tough.

Do not forget that not all side jobs will be lucrative and that some may require some time to succeed. Being patient and flexible is crucial, as is learning from your mistakes in order to develop and expand your secondary sources of income over time.

Advancing Your Career: Negotiation, Skill Building, and Networking

It takes a mix of networking, skill development, and negotiating to advance your career. What you need know about each is as follows:

How to Advance Your Career:

Define your career aspirations and where you want to go in the future by setting clear goals.

Continuous Learning: Pick up new skills and stay current on industry trends.

Request Feedback: Request feedback frequently to find areas that may be improved.

Work Ethic: In your present position, demonstrate commitment, dependability, and a good work ethic.
Identify a mentor who can offer advice and assistance.

Negotiation:

Realize Your Worth: Look into the pay ranges and benefits offered for your position in your industry and area.

Outline your negotiation strategy and the outcome you want to accomplish in advance.

In order to effectively communicate, you must be able to articulate your value, prowess, and accomplishments.

Be adaptable: Be prepared to make concessions and identify win-win solutions.

Remain Calm: Control your emotions when negotiating.

Skill Development:

Identify key skills: Decide on the key competencies that are most important in your area.

Training and Courses: To acquire these talents, spend money on seminars, courses, or certifications.

Practice: Apply your knowledge in practical settings to obtain experience.

Feedback: Seek feedback to continuously hone and enhance your abilities.

Adaptability: As sectors change, be willing to pick up new abilities.

Networking:

Create Connections: Make contact with coworkers, mentors, and business leaders.

Online Presence: Keep up a solid LinkedIn page and participate in pertinent online forums.

Attend Events: To meet individuals in your profession, go to conferences, seminars, and networking events.

Offer Value: Add value to your network by imparting your wisdom or offering help.

Action Plan: Maintain your relationships by following up frequently and communicating.

Keep in mind that developing your profession is a continuous process. Be persistent and patient since success frequently requires work and time.

Additionally, adjust your strategy as necessary to reflect your shifting objectives and situation.

Building a Business: Entrepreneurship and Financial Considerations

Planning, carrying out, and financial considerations are just a few of the many factors that go into starting a firm and becoming an entrepreneur. Here is a summary of what you should know:

Idea for a business and planning:

- Start with a clear company concept that solves a particular issue or market need.
- To better understand your target market, the competitors, and market trends, do market research.
- Make a thorough business plan that includes an outline of your objectives, strategy, and operational processes.

Legal Framework:

- Select a company legal structure, such as a corporation, LLC, partnership, or sole proprietorship. Responsibility, taxes, and ownership are impacted by this choice.

Financing:

- Choose your company's financing strategy. Options include crowdsourcing, loans, startup capital, and personal savings.
- Prepare a financial forecast that contains estimates of the start-up expenses, income, and expenses for at least the first several years.

Positioning in the market

- Create a distinctive value proposition that distinguishes your company from rivals.
- Create a distinctive brand identity for your business, including a name, a logo, and message.

Sales and marketing

- Make a marketing plan to connect with your target audience both online and offline.
- Create a sales plan to turn leads into customers and keep them as clients.

Management and Operations:

- Create effective operational procedures and processes.
- If required, hire and manage staff, and assign duties efficiently.

Compliance with laws and regulations:

- Make sure you abide by all applicable laws and rules, especially those pertaining to licenses, permits, and taxes.

Client Focus:

- Focus on client happiness and collect feedback for ongoing development.

Financial Administration:

- Keep thorough financial records and keep your personal and company funds separate.
- To make sure the company maintains its financial soundness, keep an eye on cash flow and planning.

Scaling and expansion:

- Create a growth strategy and think about increasing the range of your products and services.
- If appropriate, investigate additional markets or geographical regions.

Risk Administration

- Create a list of possible dangers to your company and put backup measures in place.
- To reduce some dangers, take into account your insurance possibilities.

Relationships and networking

- Create a network of business contacts to receive knowledge, guidance, and collaboration opportunities.

Adaptability:

- Be ready to modify your company model if necessary in order to respond to shifting market conditions.

Lifelong Education:

- By engaging in ongoing learning and professional development, you can keep up with current business trends and best practices.

Exit Technique:

- Make preparations for the potential that your company will be sold, merged, or transferred to heirs.

Keep in mind that being an entrepreneur may be difficult, and success frequently requires patience. Ask mentors, business professionals, and other entrepreneurs for guidance. To increase your chances of long-term success, constantly evaluate and tweak your company tactics.

Conclusion

Reflecting on Your Financial Journey

A crucial step in achieving financial well-being is reflection on your financial path. What you need to know is as follows:

Recognize Your Objectives: Clarify your financial objectives first. Do you want to explore the globe, pay off debt, purchase a house, or accumulate money for retirement? Your financial decisions will be influenced by your ambitions.

Obtaining Financial Data : Gather all of your financial records, such as those for your investments, bank accounts, debts, and invoices. You will have a comprehensive understanding of your financial status after reading this.

Create a Budget: To keep track of your income and spending, create a budget. This enables you to see where your money is going and where improvements to increase your savings or investments may be made.

Track Your Spending: Keep a log of your daily outgoings to see any potential areas of overspending. There are several tools and applications available to make this procedure simpler.

Debt assessment ::Examine your outstanding loans, their interest rates, and their repayment plans. Create a strategy to pay off high-interest bills as soon as you can.

Emergency fund : Make sure you have three to six months' worth of living costs set up in case of emergencies. In the event of unforeseen circumstances, it serves as a financial safety net.

Investment Review: Review your investing portfolio on a frequent basis. Make sure it fits with your risk appetite and long-term objectives. To spread risk, diversify your investments.

Saving goals : Set explicit savings objectives for your short- and long-term requirements. Automate your funds to help them last longer.

Retirement planning : Assess your retirement assets and contributions to retirement accounts like 401(k)s or IRAs as part of your retirement planning. To achieve your retirement objectives, adjust your contributions as necessary.

Review your insurance coverage, including your health, life, and property plans. Make sure your insurance is sufficient for your requirements.

Tax Efficiency: Consider the tax ramifications of your financial actions and investments. Look for lawful strategies to reduce your tax obligation.

Continue your financial education by learning more about personal money. You can use books, podcasts, and internet tools to make educated judgments.

Seek Professional Advice: If your financial position is complex, you might want to speak with a financial counselor or planner. They are able to offer specific advice.

Set milestones and organize your financial path around them. Celebrate progress along the road to keep yourself inspired.

Periodic Reflection : Regularly, or at least once a year, evaluate your financial success. As your circumstances change, modify your goals and techniques.

Keep Your Discipline: It takes patience and discipline to accumulate wealth and reach your goals. Refrain from impulsive spending and follow your budget.

Financial Well-Being: Keep in mind that financial well-being involves more than simply having money; it also involves lowering financial stress and raising your standard of living.

Stay informed: Keep an eye out for any changes in tax legislation, financial news, or economic trends that may have an influence on your money.

Support system: Talk to a dependable friend, member of your family, or your spouse about your financial path. They may support you and hold you responsible.

Avoid comparing your financial trajectory to that of others. Since every person's circumstances are different, you should compare your development to your own objectives.

Keep in mind that taking stock of your financial path is a continuous activity. It's about making wise choices, adjusting to change, and striving toward your chosen lifestyle and financial stability.

Embracing Lifelong Financial Empowerment

A key component of safeguarding your financial future and accomplishing your financial objectives is accepting lifetime financial empowerment. You should be aware of and take the following actions:

Establish Clearly Defined Financial Goals: Begin by outlining your short- and long-term financial objectives. Having specific goals will help you make better financial decisions, whether you're purchasing a home, saving for retirement, or paying off debt.

Budgeting: To keep track of your income and spending, make a monthly budget. This will enable you to make the required modifications by assisting you in understanding where your money is going.

Emergency Fund: Set up three to six months' worth of living costs in an emergency fund. This offers protection in the event of unanticipated financial losses.

Invest wisely: Learn about several investing possibilities, including stocks, bonds, real estate, and retirement accounts. Invest wisely. If you want to reduce risk and pursue long-term gain, diversify your investments.

Debt management: Create a strategy to pay off any debt you may have. Prioritize debts with high interest rates and think about combining or refinancing to reduce interest rates.

Continue your financial education by learning more about personal money. Books, online classes, and seminars may all offer insightful information.

Contribute to retirement accounts like 401(k)s and IRAs as part of your retirement planning. Start as soon as you can to benefit from compound interest.

Insurance Coverage: Ensure you have adequate health, house, vehicle, and life insurance. It offers defense against unforeseen circumstances.

Tax Planning: Recognize the tax ramifications of your financial choices and investigate ways to reduce your tax obligations.

Review Your Finances Frequently: Monitor the development of your financial objectives. To stay on course, modify your strategy as necessary.

Seek Professional Advice: To receive individualized advice on your financial position, think about speaking with a financial counselor or planner.

Avoid Impulsive Spending: Exercise restraint and refrain from making rash decisions. Save for significant costs and put necessities before desires as a priority.

Create Multiple Income Streams: Look for ways to make extra money, including side jobs, investments, or passive income sources.

Estate planning : Establish a strategy for the distribution of your assets in the event that you die away by creating or updating your will.

Stay Informed: Keep up with economic and financial news that might affect your investments or financial decisions to stay informed.

Mindset and Behavior :Understand the psychological components of effective money management. Recognize your spending patterns and practice financial restraint.

Join financial forums or support groups to exchange experiences and gain knowledge from others. Network.

Remain patient since it takes time to accumulate riches and become financially independent. Be patient and persistent in pursuing your financial objectives.

Keep in mind that achieving financial independence is a journey, and it's OK to ask for assistance and modify your tactics along the way. The secret is to manage your finances in a proactive, knowledgeable, and disciplined manner throughout your whole life.

www.ingramcontent.com/pod-product-compliance
Lightning Source LLC
Chambersburg PA
CBHW062331290526
45794CB00005B/1990